# No-one is boı ... scared of the dentist

A new born baby and very young children know nothing about dentists.

But as they grow up they're learning all the time - to speak, relate to others, colour a picture. But they can also learn to be scared. You see it all the time when a parent passes on a fear.

- Spiders
- Heights
- Wasps
- Swimming/water
- Food

...the list could go on forever.

*"But I've never told them to be scared…"*

Some children are naturally more anxious or avoidant than others. But how we react can make that either worse - or better.

Children are great at reading people. They see how we stand, what we say, how we look and speak. They'd make great detectives.

# SO WHAT ARE YOU PASSING ON?

...good stuff that helps
- or bad stuff that makes things worse?

# It's a vicious cycle

Things you think can affect how you feel and what you do. So if you are scared, your child can pick it up even when you think you're doing your best to cover it up.

If you predict going to the dentist will be hard and you're scared about how you or they will react, then an unhelpful cycle can occur where scary thoughts lead to scary emotions which are uncomfortable. Strong emotions can get the adrenaline going leading to unpleasant physical reactions. And all this can add up to *alter what you do*.

So, what might someone do when they're feeling scared of something? They avoid things, put it off, make excuses, sweep it under the carpet.

# This book is about setting up healthier patterns

So that visiting the dentist is a normal and routine part of a healthy life.

Ready to get started?

Let's do some introductions

READ A
STORY
TOGETHER

# Use story-time to help them prepare

Children come in all sorts of shapes and sizes. They have different personalities too. A helpful and healthy reaction for youngsters is to be wary of strangers. Many toddlers grab hold of their parent and won't venture far away from home base when they meet unfamiliar people.

So the key is to start to make going to the dentist familiar. How?

Why not read a book?

There are some great, attractive and friendly books about visiting the dentist.

For example:
• Usborne books, and also the "Peppa Pig: Dentist trip" are two examples of books about visiting the dentist.

Talking about the dentist can also help your child feel safe.

It can help to be able to describe who your child will meet.

# MEET THE TEAM

They're all there to help.

## ◀ The dentist

The tooth expert. They are there to help you have healthy teeth and gums.

## ◀ The hygienist

Helps the dentist and may also polish your teeth so they're clean or apply a fluoride varnish.

## The nurse ▶

Sits beside you helping the dentist get a great view of your teeth - say "Cheese!" They also make notes of how your teeth are looking.

## ◀ Receptionist

Sits at the front desk and arranges appointments.

# GO MAKE AN APPOINTMENT

## To Do

- Feed cat
- Buy milk
- Go to bank
- Book appointment at the Dentist

# Make that call

It's tempting to avoid things that seem difficult. That's why you might be tempted to put off going to the dentist with your child if you think it will be a difficult visit.

This may be understandable - and might make you both feel happier at the time, but it doesn't help either of you in the long term.

Going for regular check-ups stops problems developing and helps prevent treatment being needed. Putting things off means more treatment, more appointments and more hassle for your child in the future. Or maybe infected gums, extractions and fillings.

The saying "a stitch in time" is certainly true of getting expert help from a dentist. But don't swing to the other extreme where you anxiously talk about going all the time and puts your worries into your child's head.

**What does your child need?**

# NO BIG EXPLANATIONS

# Keep it short

Make a plan of what you're going to say, and when you're going to say it.

**What are you going to say?** Tell it like it is and keep it factual "We're going to the dentist next Tuesday morning to get our teeth checked".

**When are you going to do it?** You know your child best. Would they like more notice - in which case let them know a week before. Then remind them the evening before. Or if you think they are better with a shorter period of notice, tell them the day before.

The key is tell the truth and avoid surprises on the day. Be clear what is happening. The important thing is not to lie as you'll lose trust and credibility for the future. Also, bigger things like an extraction need more time for most children to think it through - so make sure you give them at least 24 hours notice.

**When you're tempted to cancel.** If your child seems scared and says they don't want to go, you might have second thoughts about attending. Keep the appointment anyway, and let your dentist know your child is anxious.

Cancelling teaches the wrong message that you deal with anxious fears by running away. Instead they need to discover that the visit is far better than you or they feared. If you're unsure, phone your dentist and ask about what's going to happen.

Or maybe it's you who is more anxious than your child. If so, perhaps someone else should take them along - like a grandparent. Allowing someone else to take them might be a good short term solution.

# BUT BEFORE YOU GO ADD SOME DETAIL TO YOUR PLAN

# What do you need to pack?

Okay, it's not a trip away, but there are things to take that will help when you're there by providing a focus for your child. Depending on their age this might be a:

- Toy.
- Book.
- Music player (with earphones).
- Game.
- Comic.
- Something they love.

Plus a bottle of water - because not everyone likes the pink juice they give you to swill round your mouth.

But before you set off, now's the time to think what you want to ask for.

What to ask for

# Help your child write
# a letter to your dentist

Be clear about what you and
your child are asking for.

Examples:
If my child gets upset, can I…

- [ ] Talk to them?
- [ ] Continue the examination while they sit on my knee?
- [ ] Ask for what you or they need?
- [ ] Ask you to stop?
- [ ] Ask a question?
- [ ] Cuddle them/Hold their hand?

Write in any other ideas here:

-----------------------------------------------------

-----------------------------------------------------

-----------------------------------------------------

-----------------------------------------------------

Often dentists like to talk directly to the child. It shows they are interested, and builds a relationship. To help your dentist, tell them about your child so they can ask more.

My child likes ---------------------------------------

Sport - played or watched ---------------------------

The name of the school/nursery - or favourite teacher ---------------------------------------------

Any trips out from school ---------------------------

Music - artist, group or track they love

---------------------------------------------------

Names of friends ---------------------------------

Names of pets ------------------------------------

Names of siblings --------------------------------

Where they went/are going on holiday

---------------------------------------------------

# USE YOUR IMAGINATION

## Technical term

| |
|---|
| Examination. |
| Using a probe to touch or scrape teeth. |
| Recording tooth condition. This is where the dentist calls out various codes and numbers describing the different teeth. These are recorded in the dental records so your dentist can keep track of progress. |
| Using an air puffer to blow away saliva. |
| Antiseptic mouth wash. |
| Paint/varnish. |

# Find fun ways to explain what to expect

Your dentist may well have great ways of explaining what's happening. There should be no surprises. The way to make sure that's the case is to explain everything clearly.

Here are some everyday words that get rid of the jargon. You or your dentist will need to gauge what words are needed for different ages. Explain things in the correct language for your child.

| Very young child (e.g. toddler) | Older child (e.g. at school) |
|---|---|
| Have a look/Have a nosie. | Have a look. |
| Tooth tickler. | Having a good look. |
| Count the teeth. | Dental Maths. |
| Choo choo train puffer. | Drying the tooth so the dentist can see it. |
| Pink juice. | Mouth wash. |
| Painting the tooth with superhero toothpaste. | Putting on dental armour/ tooth protector. |

# DON'T RUSH

## - Calm it down

**Give yourself plenty of time**

**Arrive**

**Say hello**

**Take a seat**

**Play a game**

**Read a comic**

**Listen to music**

# THINGS YOU

## Helpful things

Have normal conversations.

Chat about a holiday or a hobby.

Talk about nursery or school.

Play some music.

Listen to an audio book.

Play with a toy.

Say they are doing a good job and being clever.

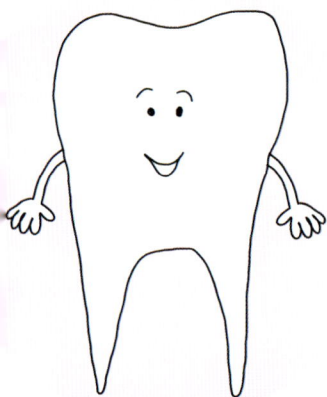

**Speak up for the Honest Tooth**

Remember to pack a music player, headphones, books, favourite toy, comforters.

# DO AND SAY

## Unhelpful things

You need to be brave.

You need to sit still.

Don't be scared.

Don't touch anything.

They're not going to hurt you.

I hate the dentist- but you'll be fine.

It will be over in five minutes.

You'll lose all your teeth/look like grand-dad.

You've got to be a big boy or girl.

They'll think you're naughty.

You won't be getting anything done.

It won't be sore.

**Don't encourage Bad Thoughts**

Try not to be angry, threatening or manipulative. It won't help.

**On the day**

# WELL DONE, YOU'VE GOT THERE

# Let the dentist help

Now's the time for you to sit down and relax. Let the dentist do their job.

Don't hover and don't try to take over. Take a seat and let the dentist do their work.

Read a book, check your texts or social media, or listen to music. If you have a phone with apps, now's the time to play a favourite game.

Trust them to do their job as a professional.

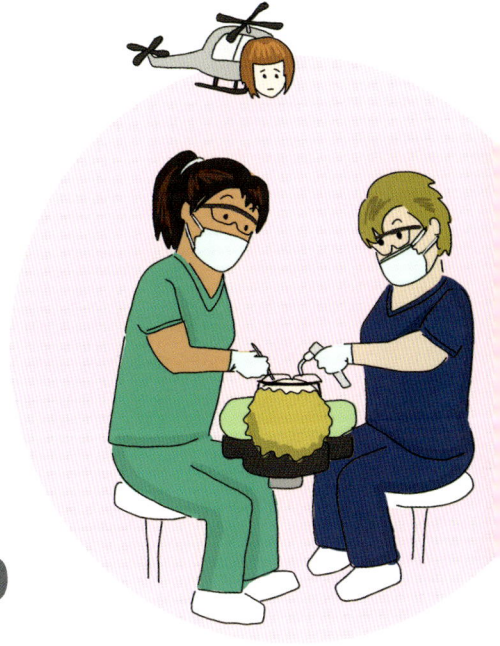

# TAKE
# A SEAT

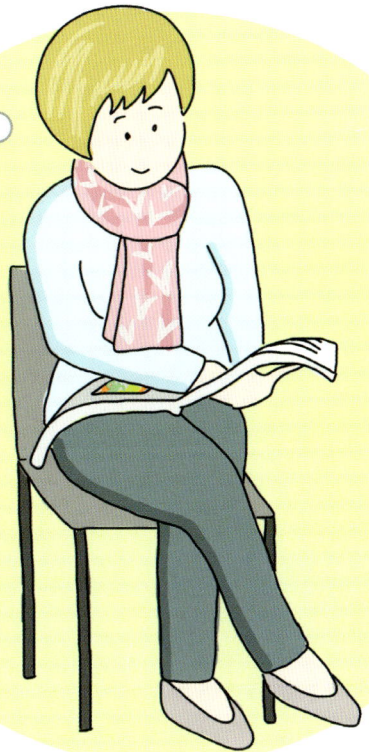

Where was the Titanic built?

# It's okay to ask questions

You'll probably want to come into the room with your child.

Even if you or they feel anxious, play it cool.

- Sit on your hands if you have to.
- Root your feet to the floor.
- Read your own magazine.
- It's also fine for you to read a magazine in the waiting room if you feel anxious.

**Remember: Act relaxed - even if you're not**

27

On the day

# WELL DONE

# Time for a small reward once they've finished

We're not talking a holiday abroad, a new bike or a pet. What about:

- A new book?
- Buy a magazine or comic?
- Or a set of colouring pencils?
- Time to watch a favourite DVD or programme?
- Play a new game or app?
- Have a friend over for a sleepover to visit?
- Go for a takeaway meal that evening?
- Have something nice for tea?
- Make them their favourite meal?

Write your child's reward in here…

---------------------------------

What about something for you?

---------------------------------

P.S. - One thing not to say is that they've been brave. You might tell them they've been clever though-because they've made a good choice getting that check-up or treatment.

# PLANNING FOR NEXT TIME

Before you leave, ask your dentist what to expect next time. Write it down so you don't forget.

------------------------------------

------------------------------------

------------------------------------

Next do a review. What went well - or less well? What would you both like to change?

------------------------------------

------------------------------------

------------------------------------

What would you do differently?

------------------------------------

------------------------------------

------------------------------------

Knowing these things will help you prepare so you're both ready when you arrive for that next appointment.

# SOME MORE HINTS AND TIPS FOR YOU AND YOUR CHILD

# Next time in the waiting room

Some things people say have helped them stay calm include:

Breathing: close your eyes and breath in time with the waves on a beach… in… and out.

Squeezing a stress ball - "how hard can you squeeze it?"

Have a workout - get your legs stretching out on the chair.

Count the time in your head - or do some tricky times tables or the alphabet if they are older.

Distract yourself with things in the waiting room e.g. a TV or magazine.

Play the game - get mining and don't forget the TNT.

Sing a song in your head, or listen to music.

Repeat positive coping statements.

Say a prayer.

and so on.

# HOW TO GET EVEN MORE HELP

There's some good information available